# Color My World
# EXOTIC BIRDS
## Coloring Book

*Inquries can be sent to colormyworld@gmx.us*

## By James Colvin

*This coloring book is dedicated to my sister Ann. She suggested I make a coloring book, so I did. Exotic Birds contains designs that will inspire you, and bring out your inner artist.*

*Whether you color for relaxation, or for creative expression, you're sure to enjoy Exotic Birds adult coloring book.*

Book Design: James Colvin
Cover Art: James Colvin
Illustrations By: James Colvin

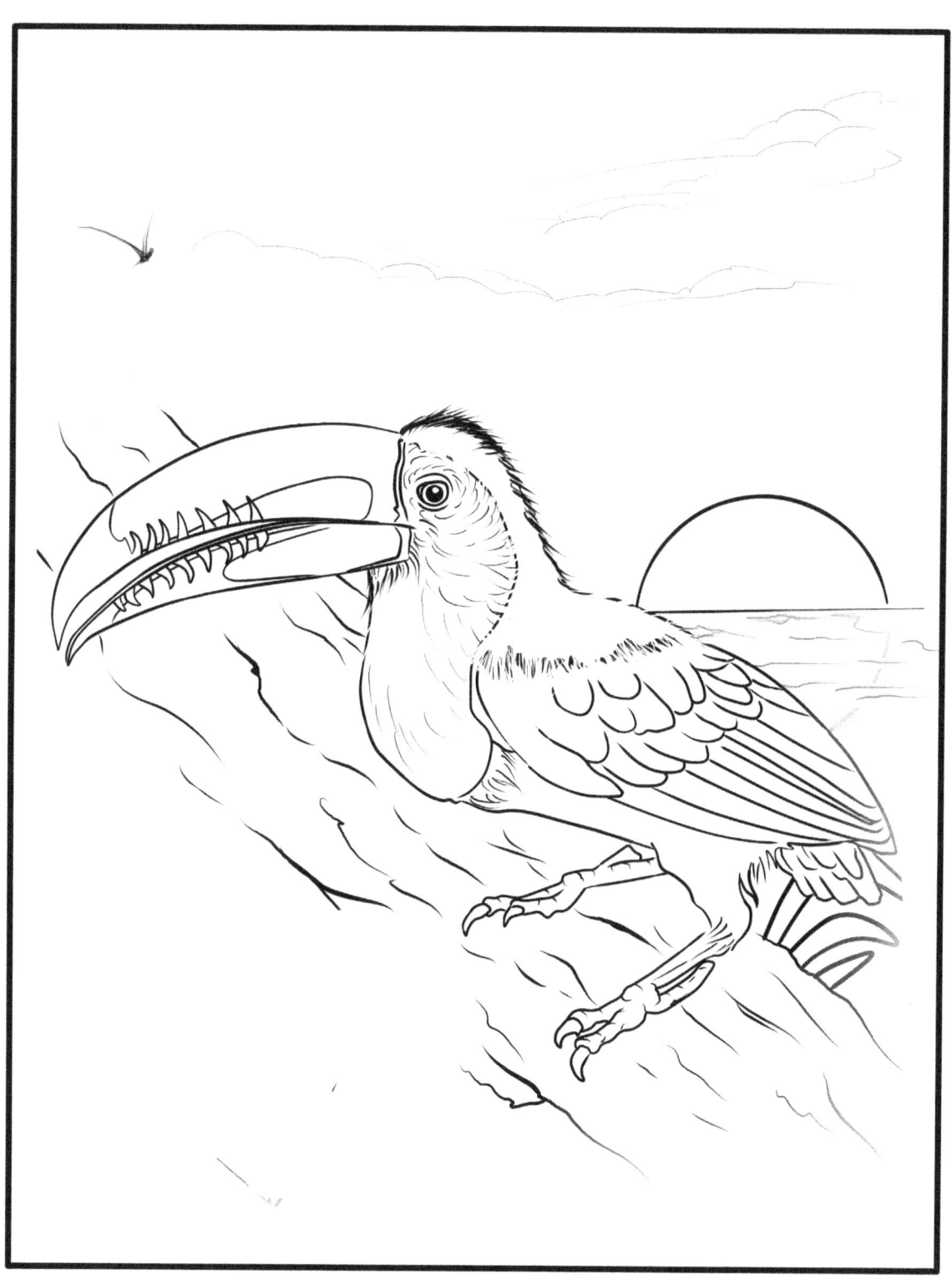

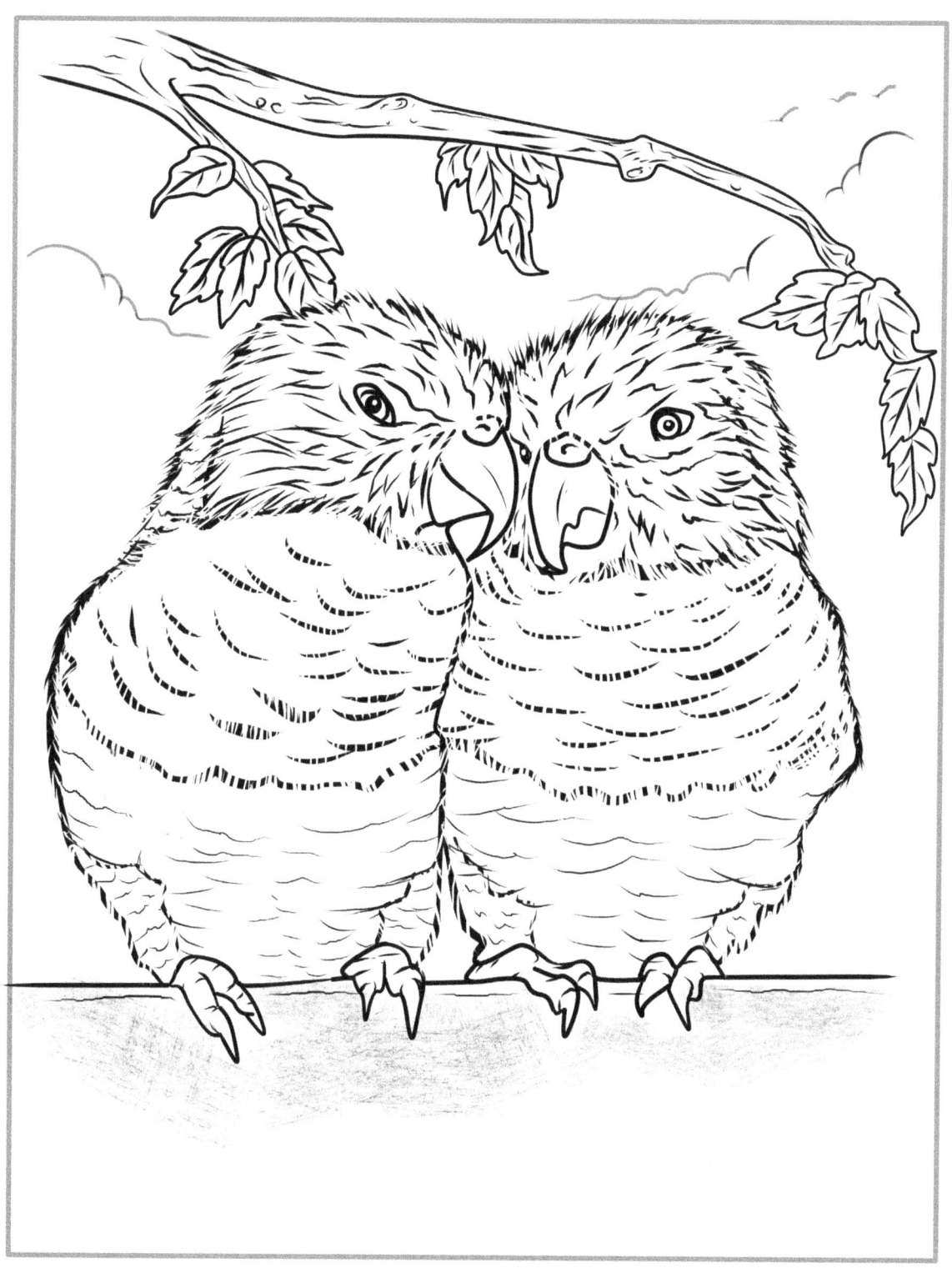

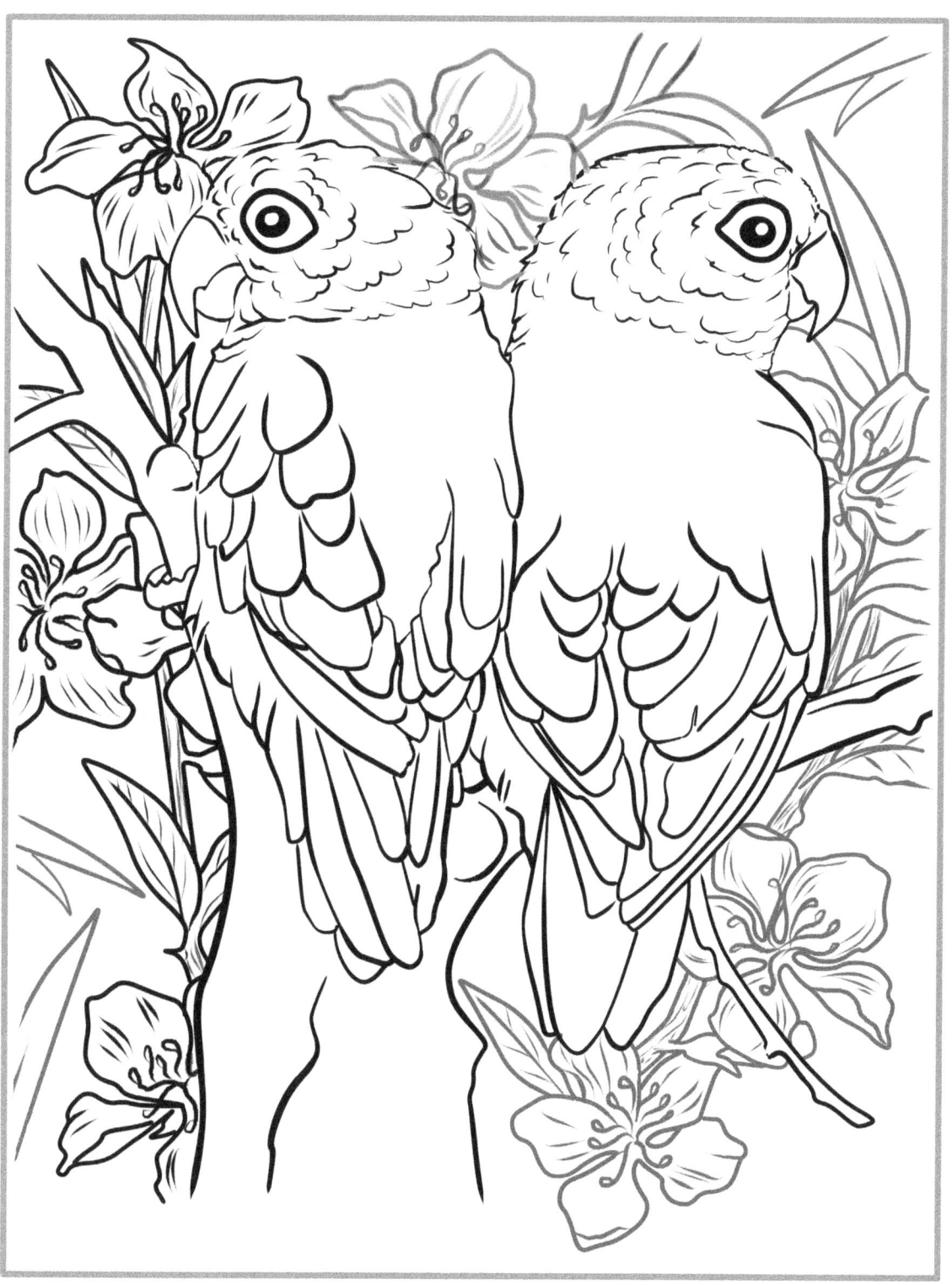

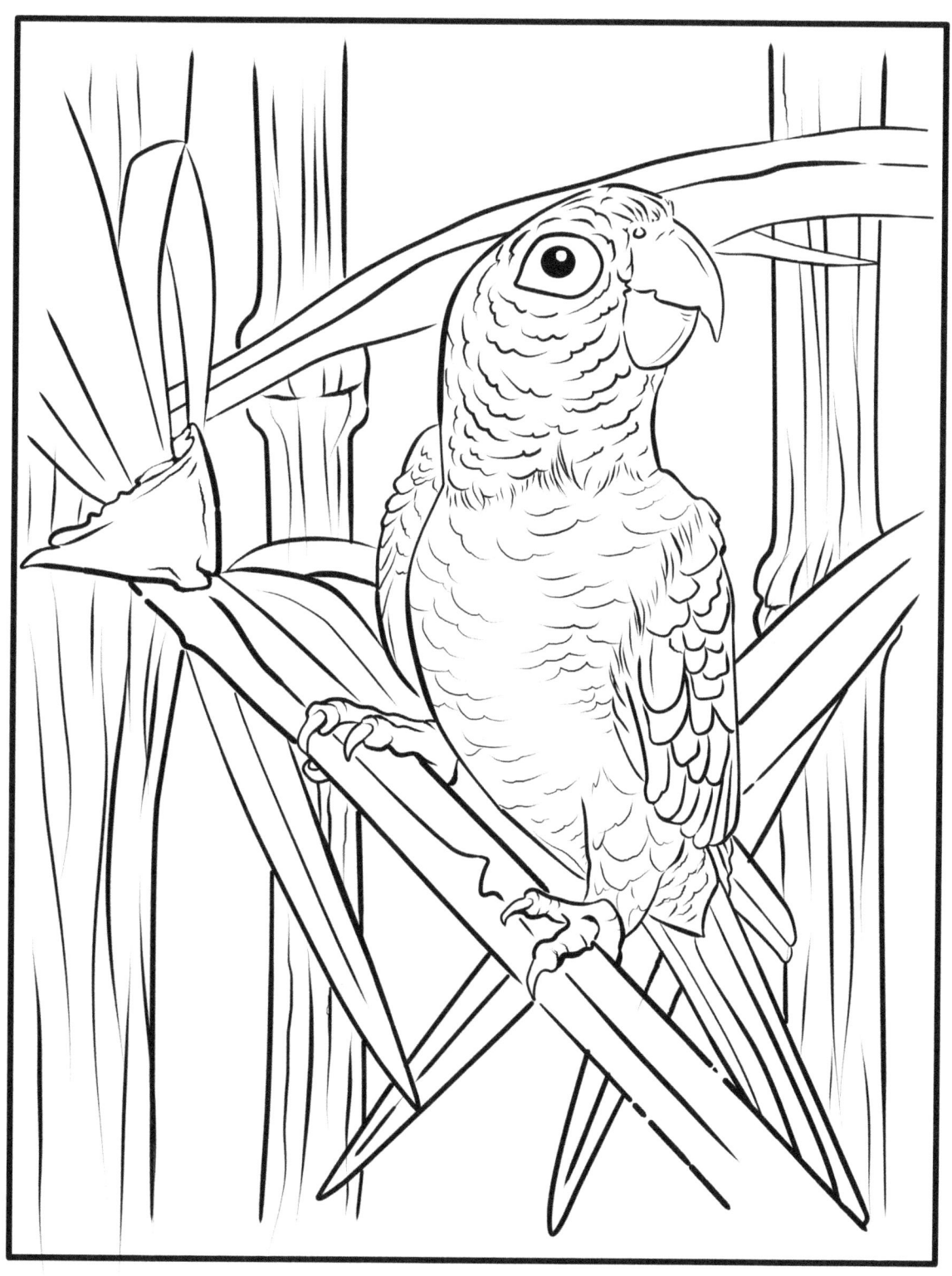

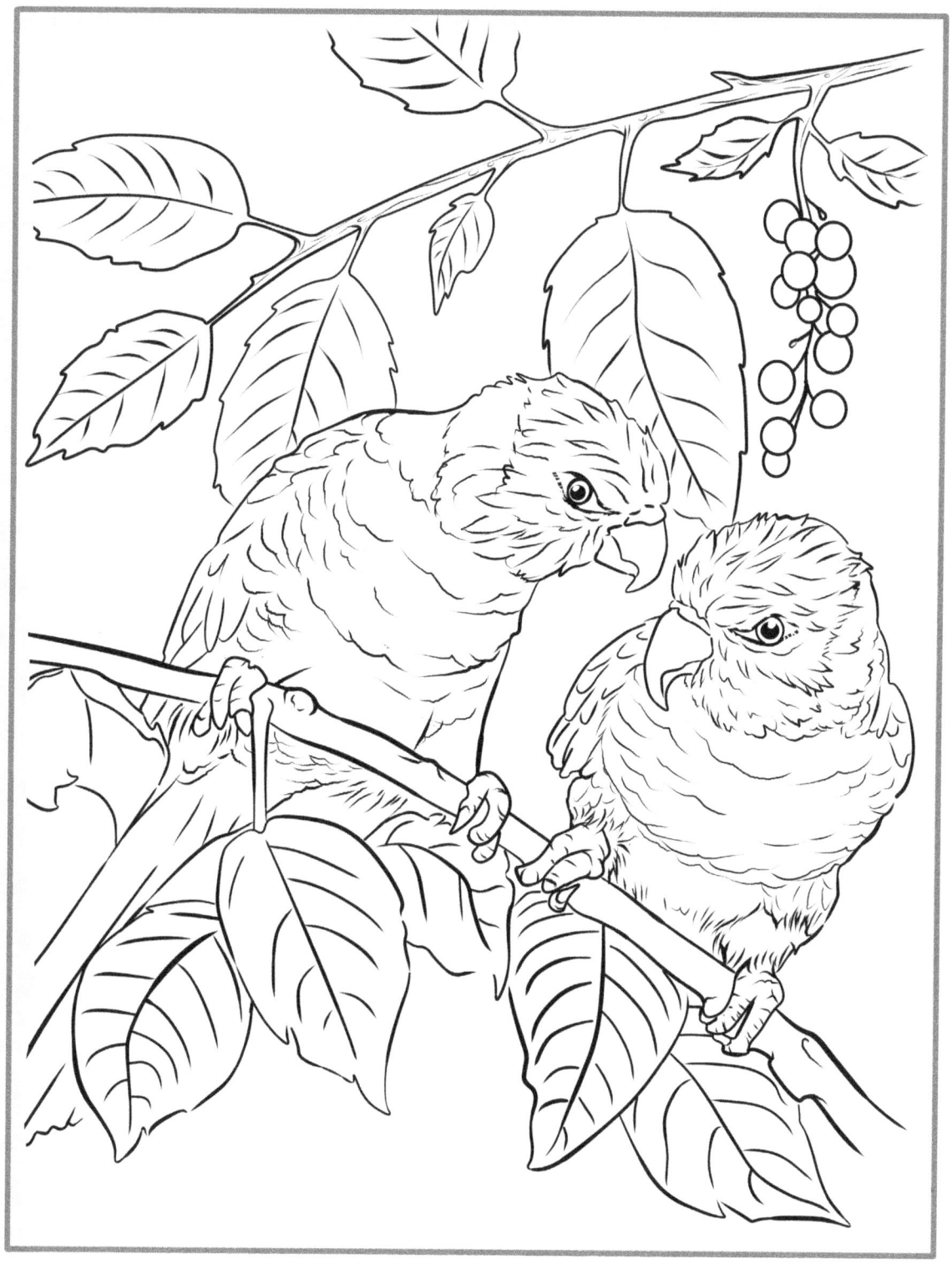

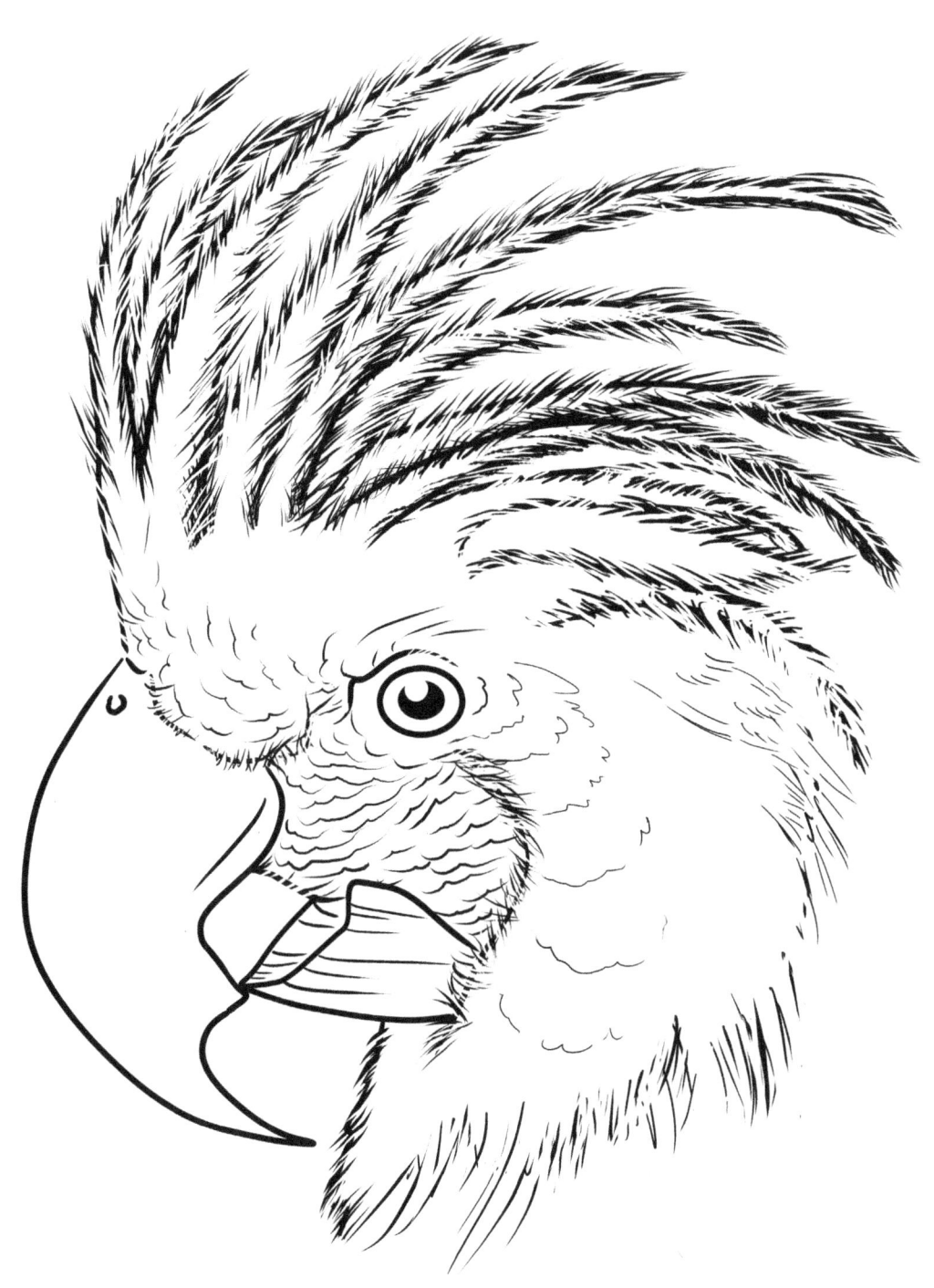

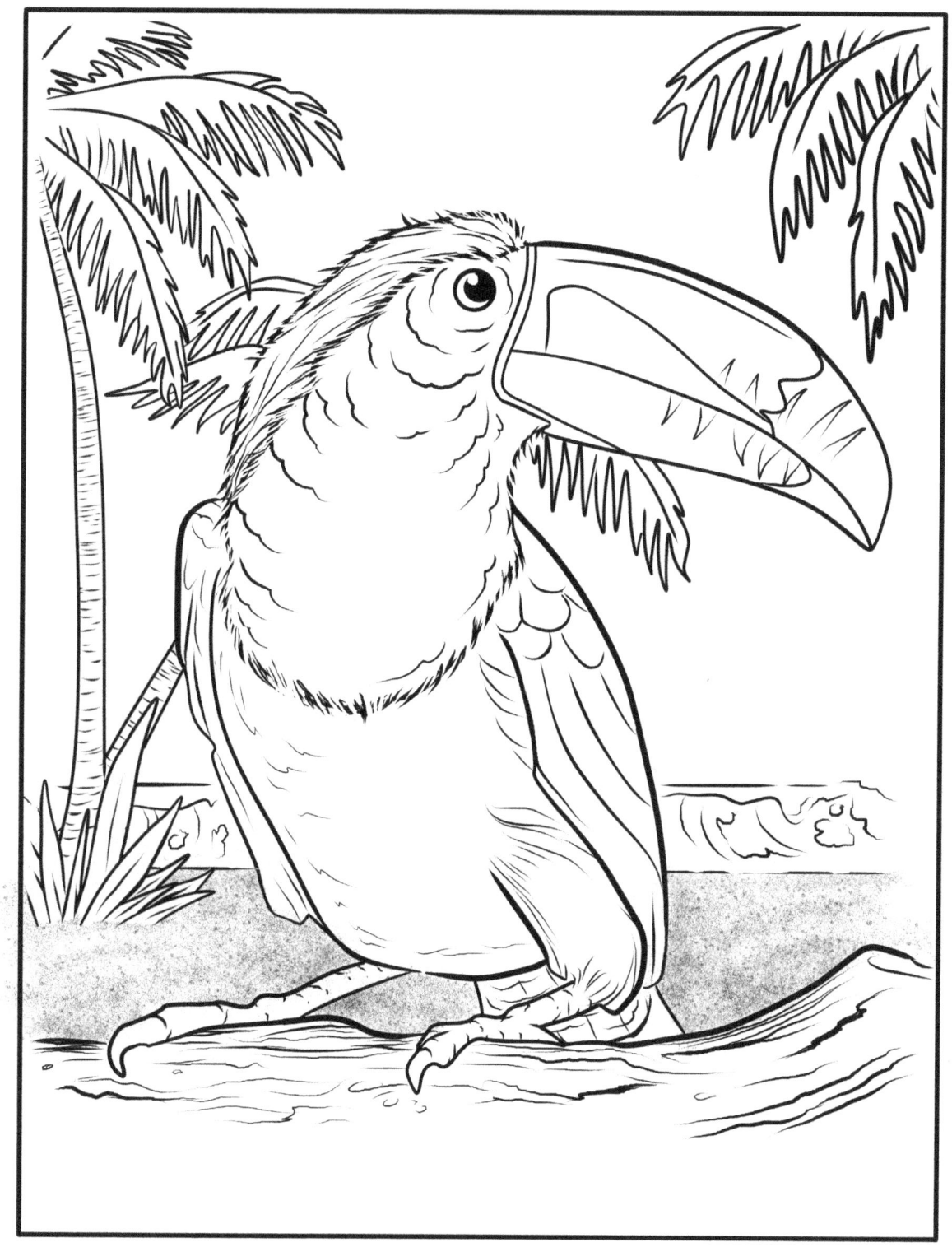

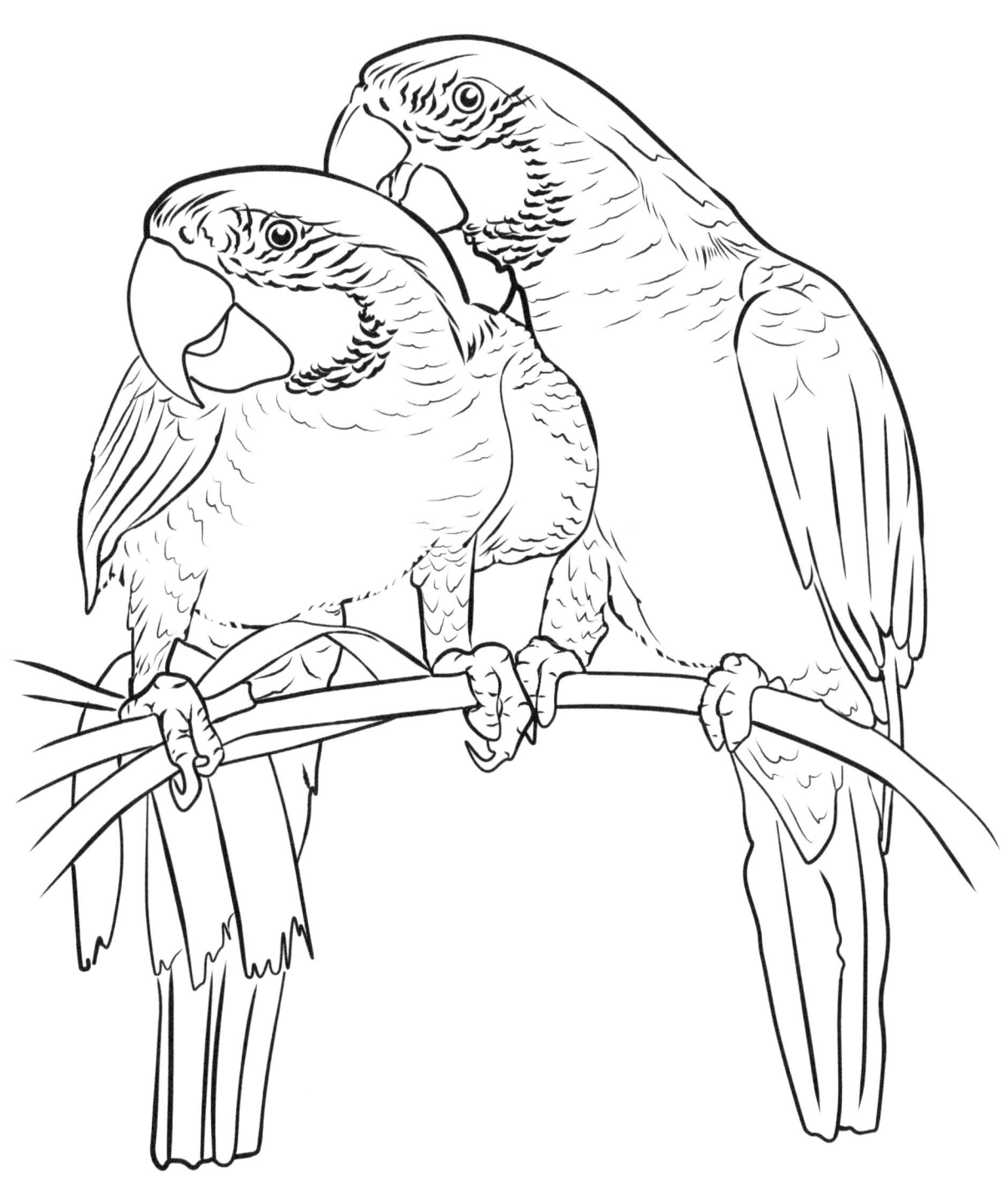

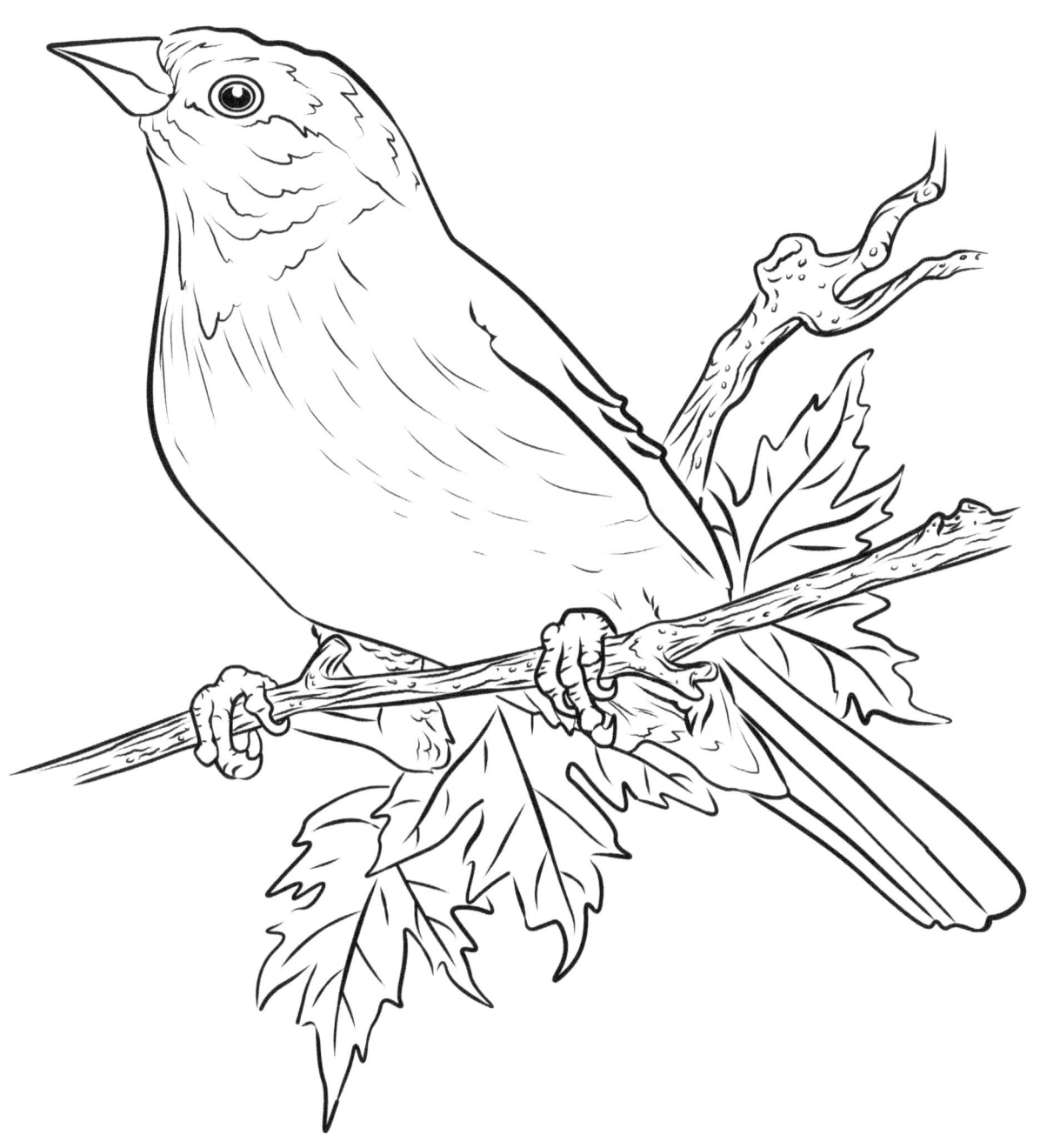

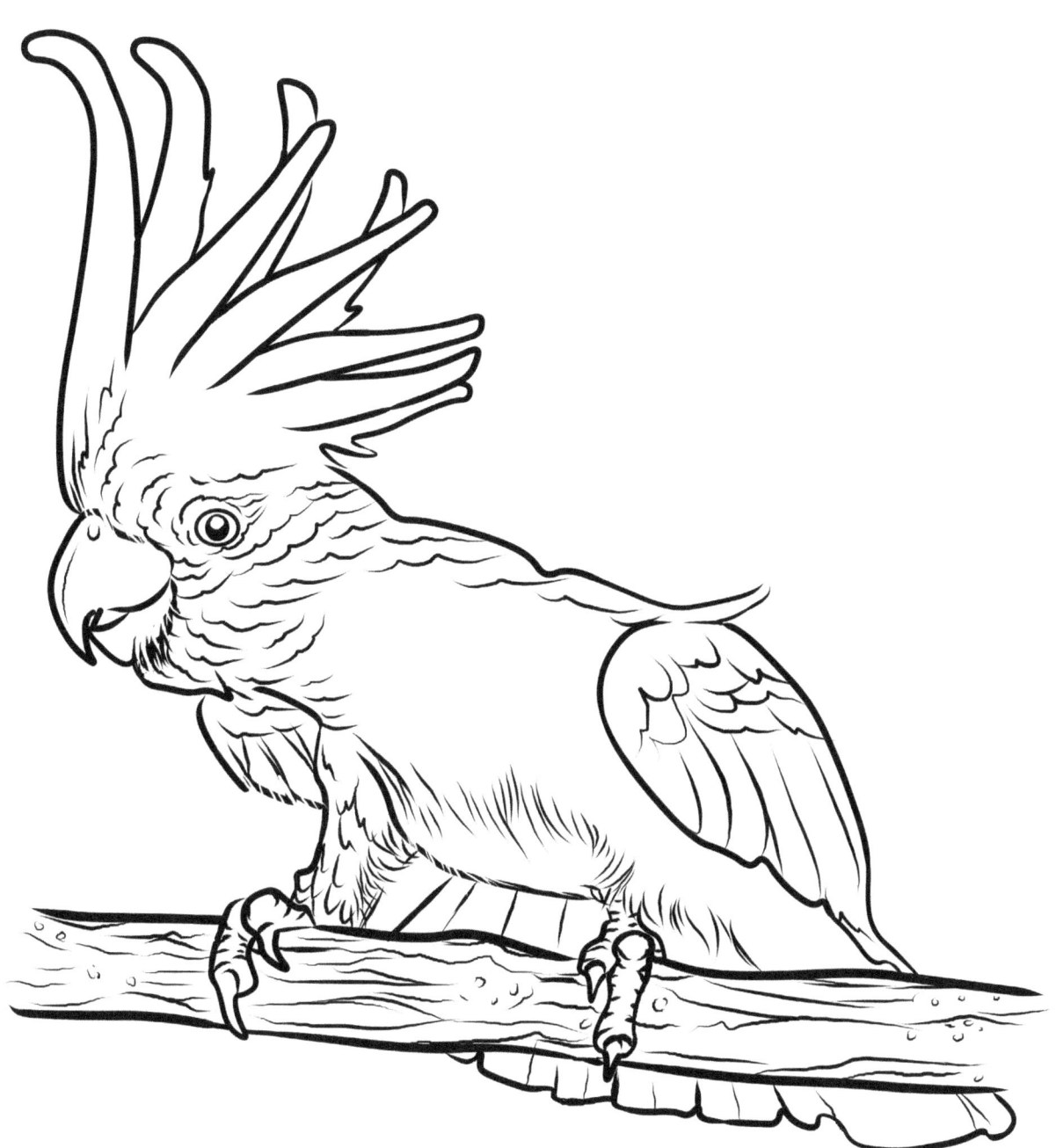

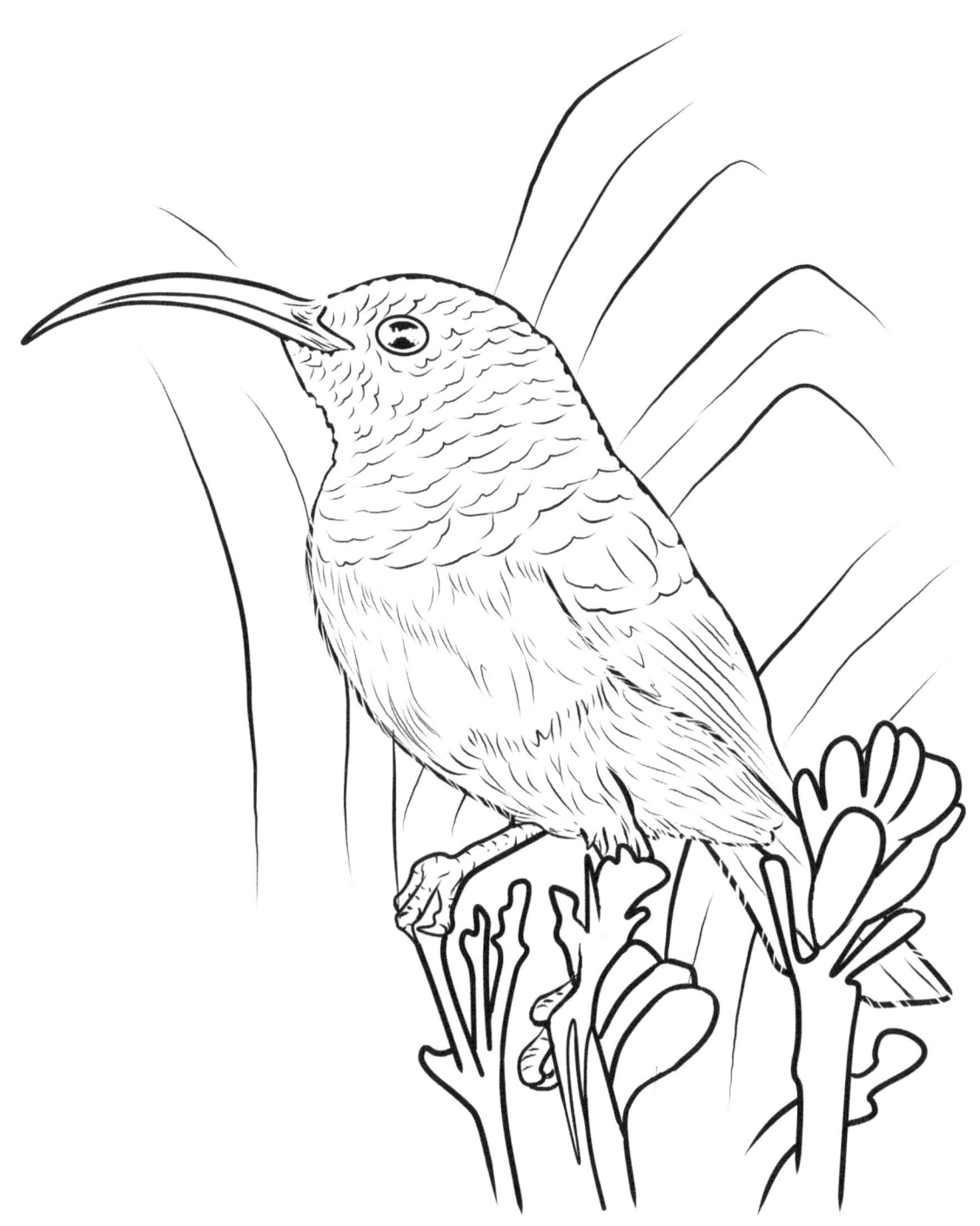

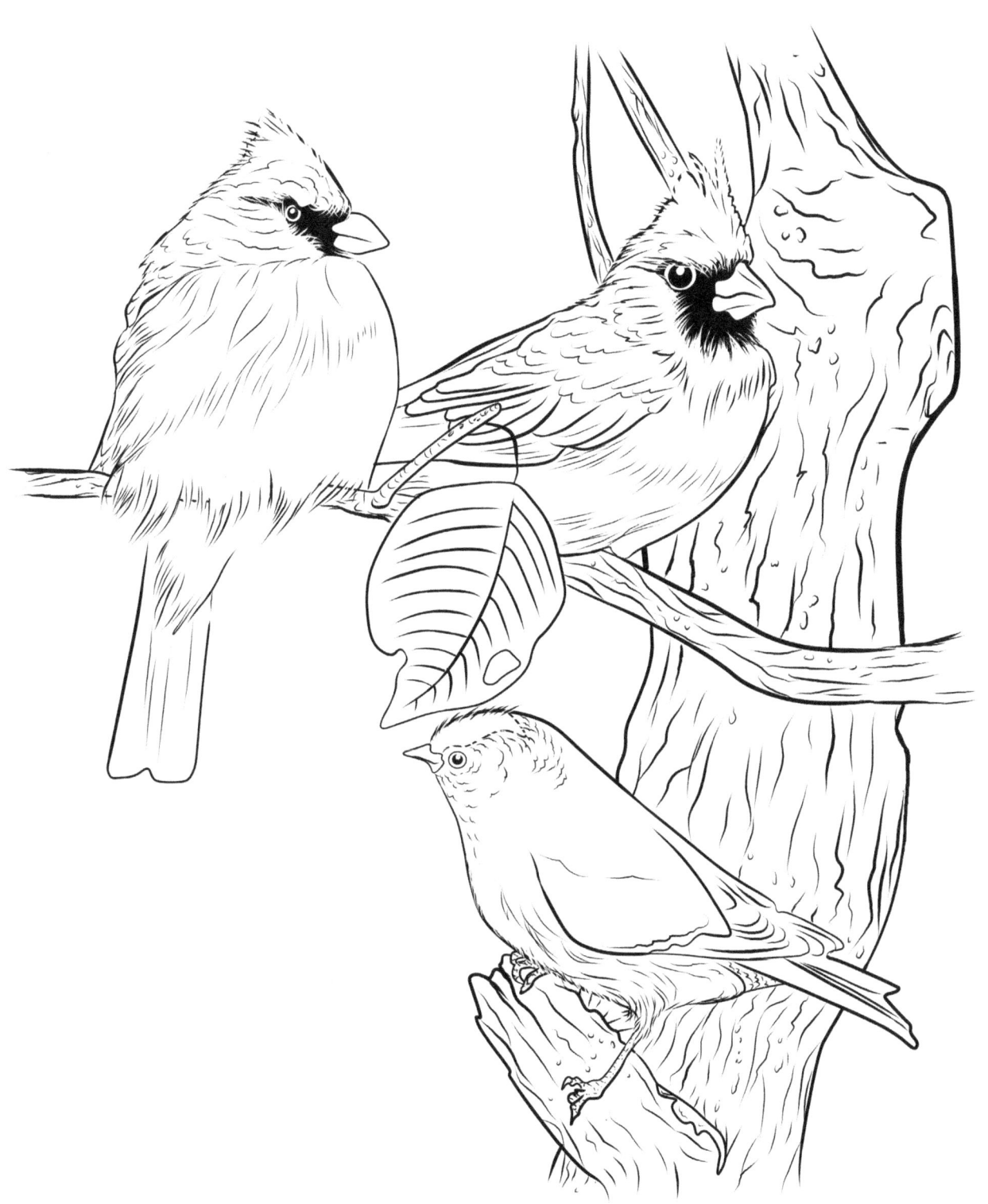

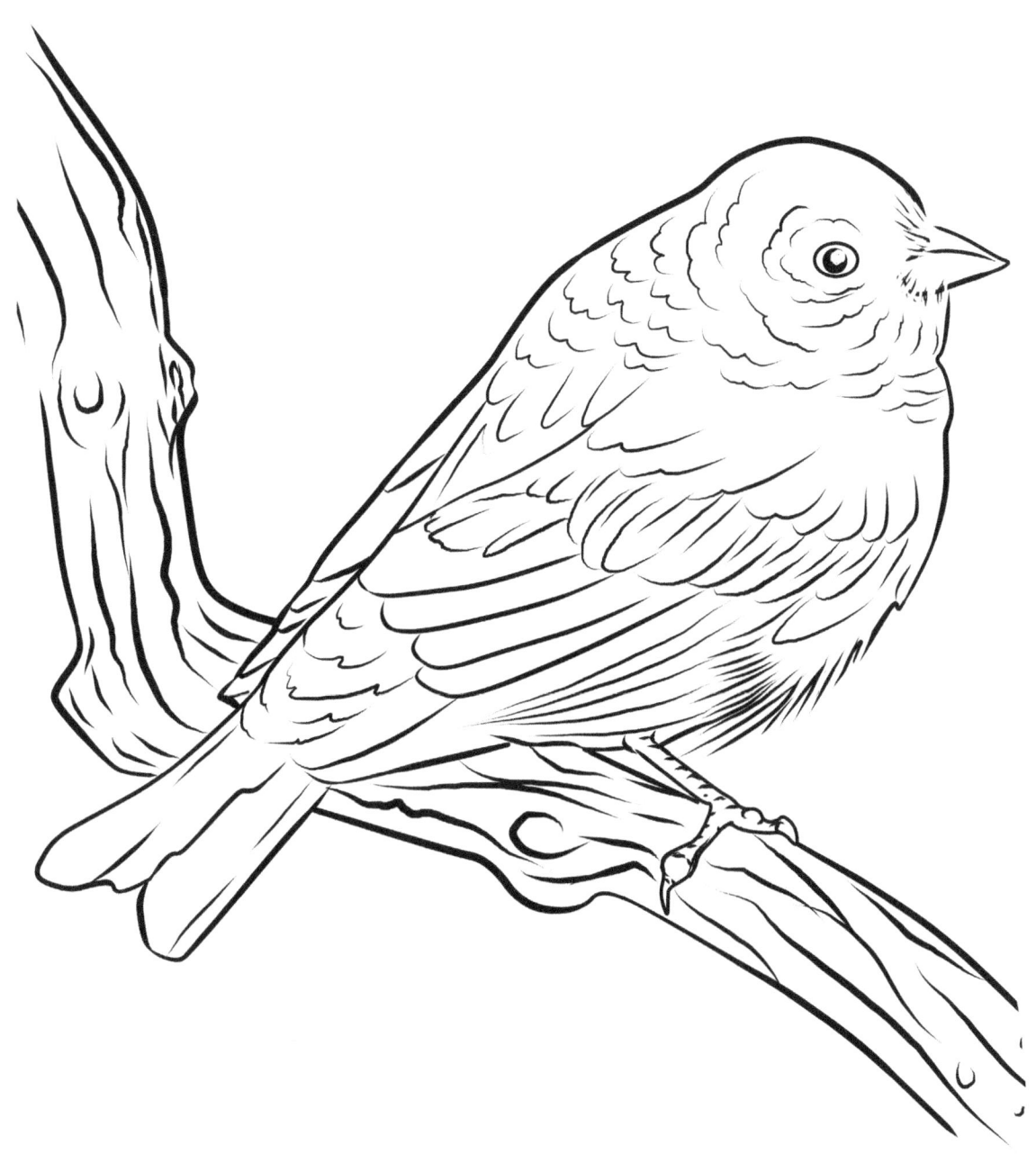

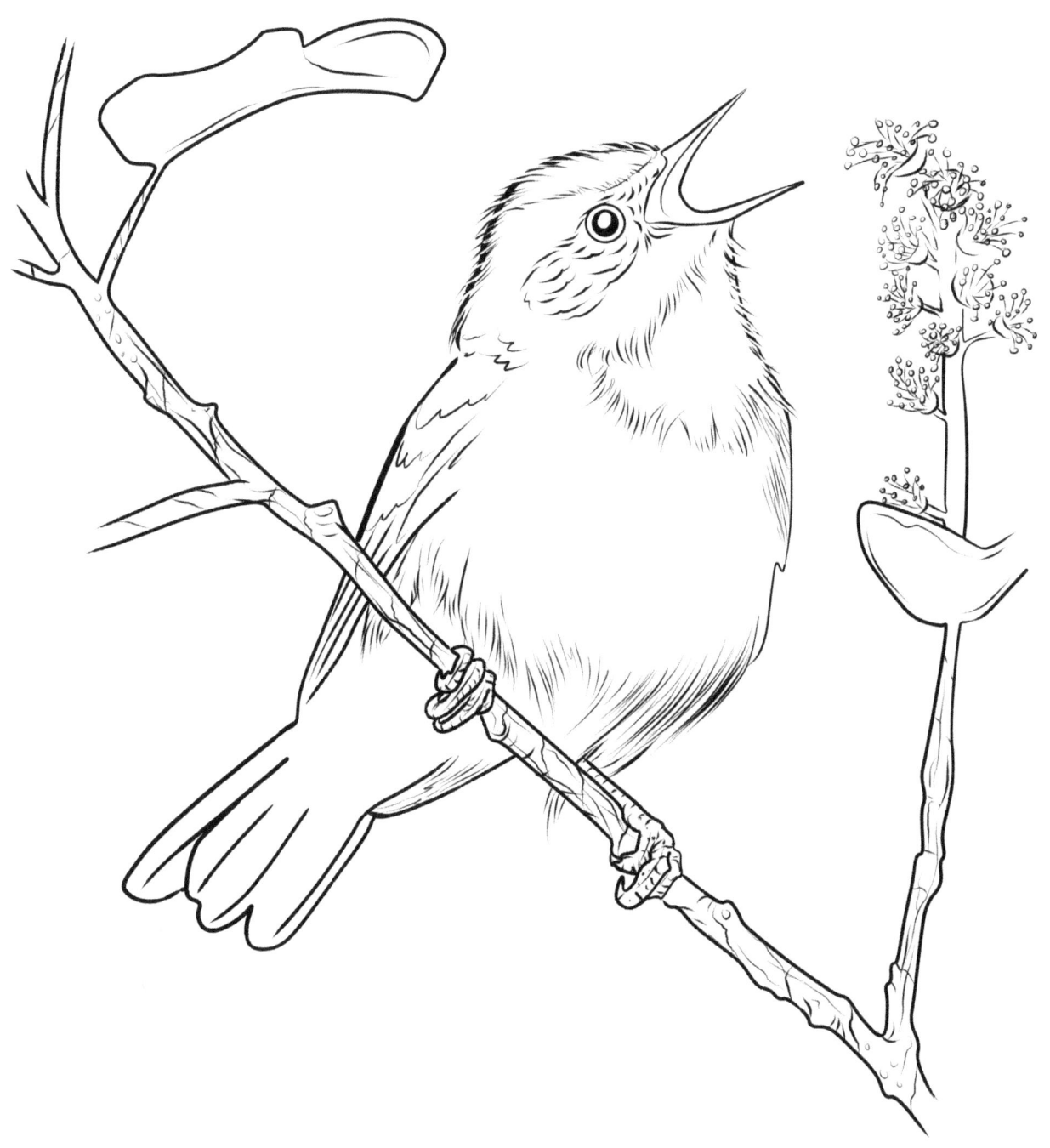

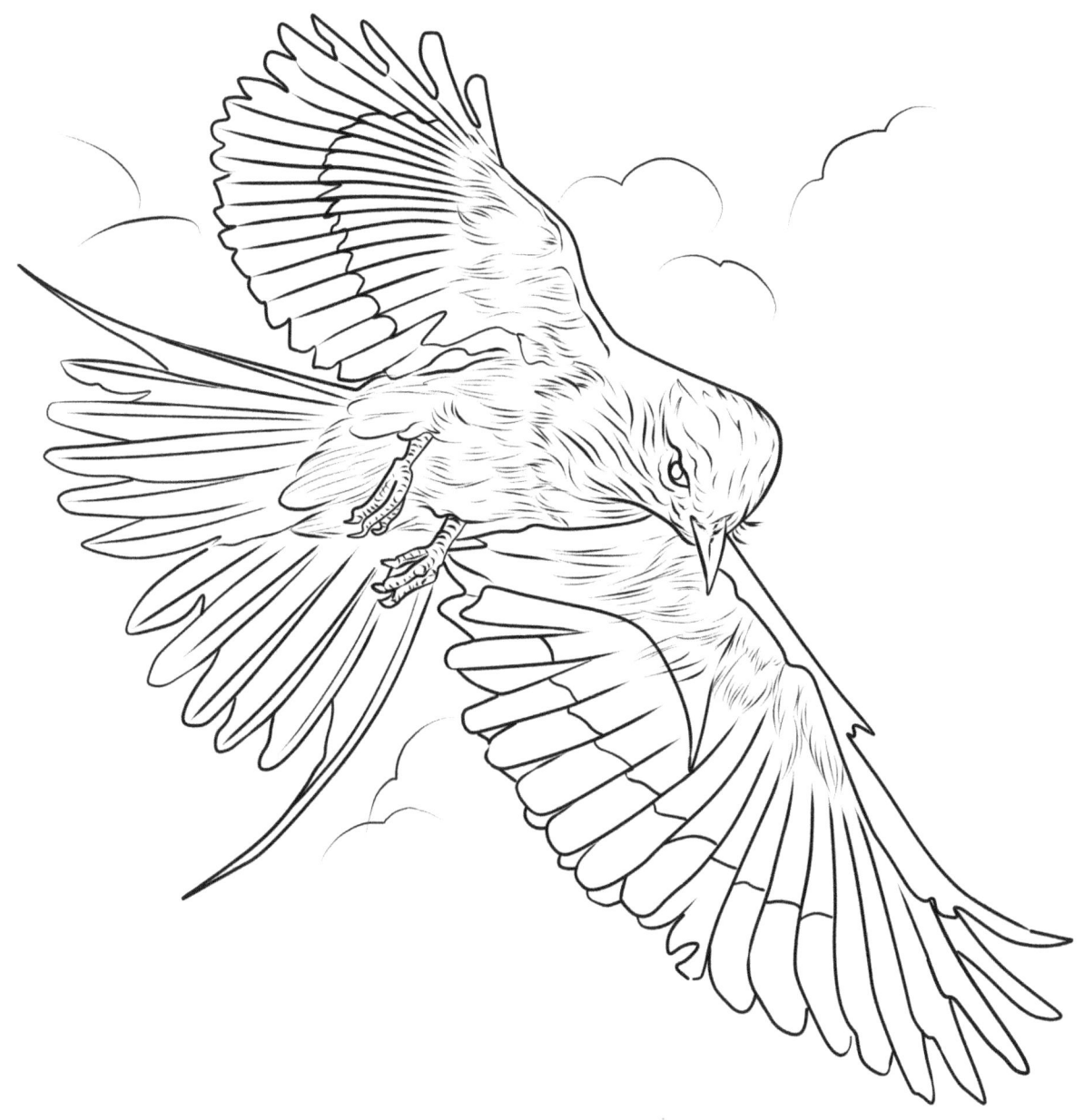

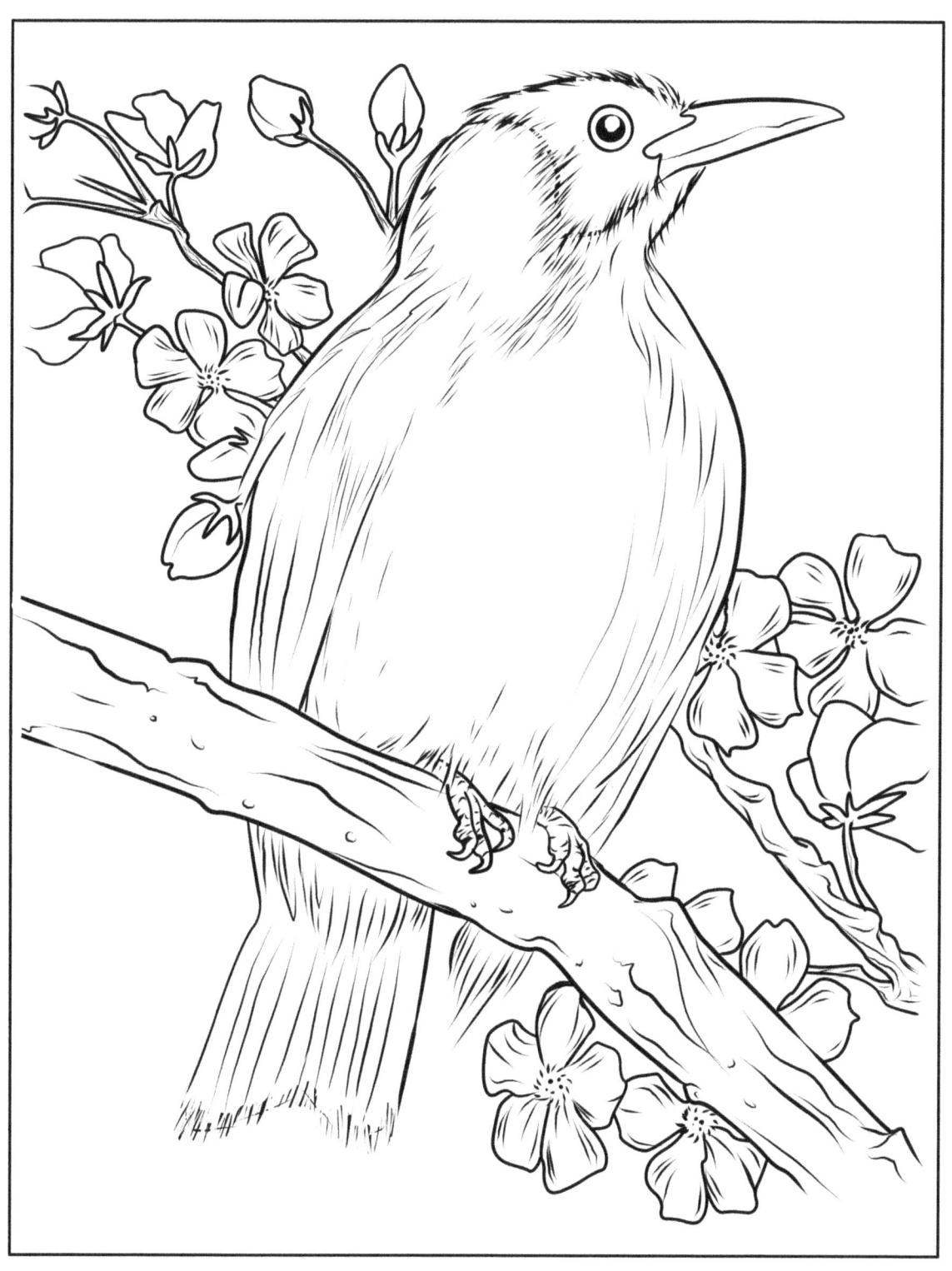

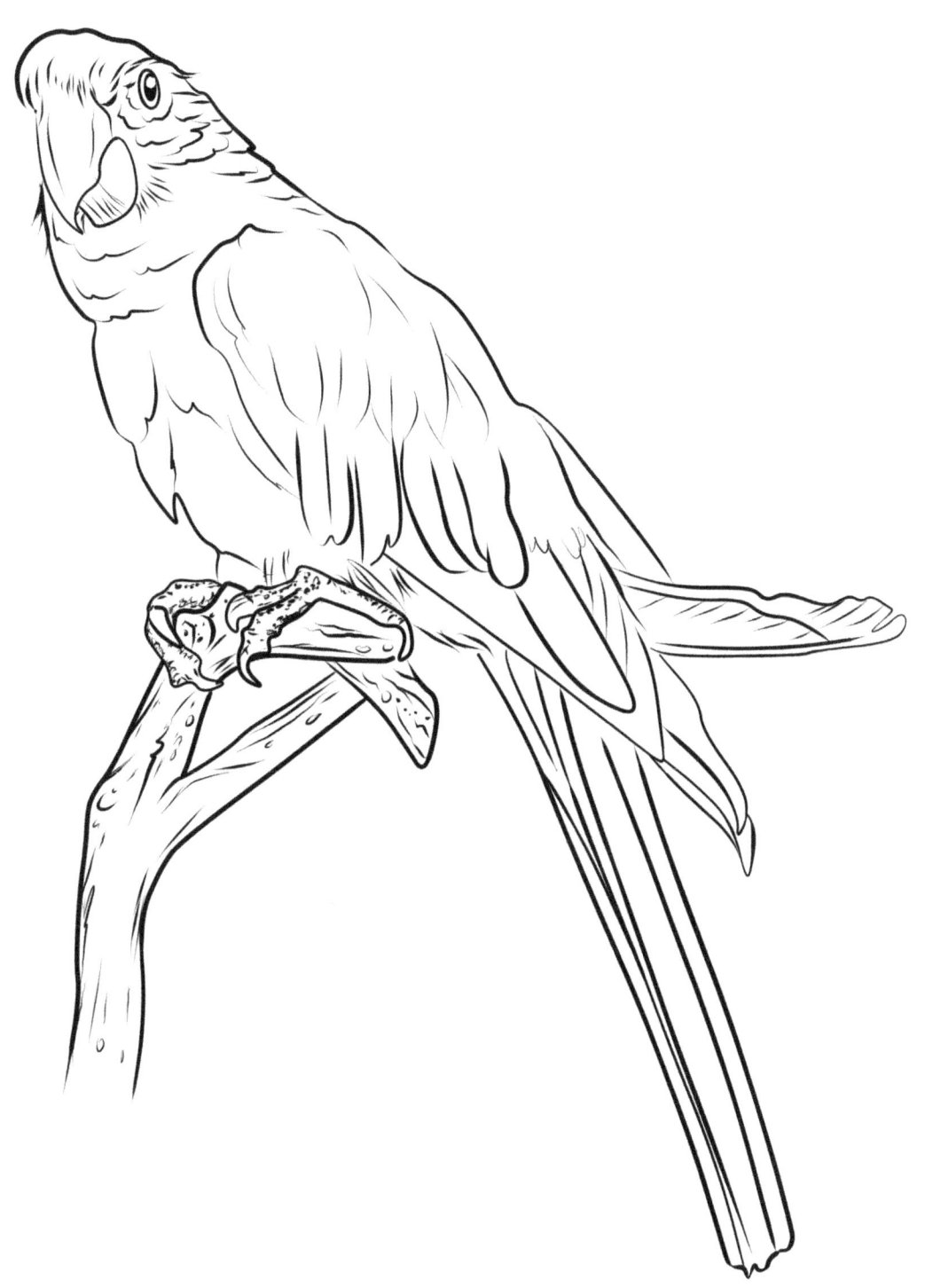

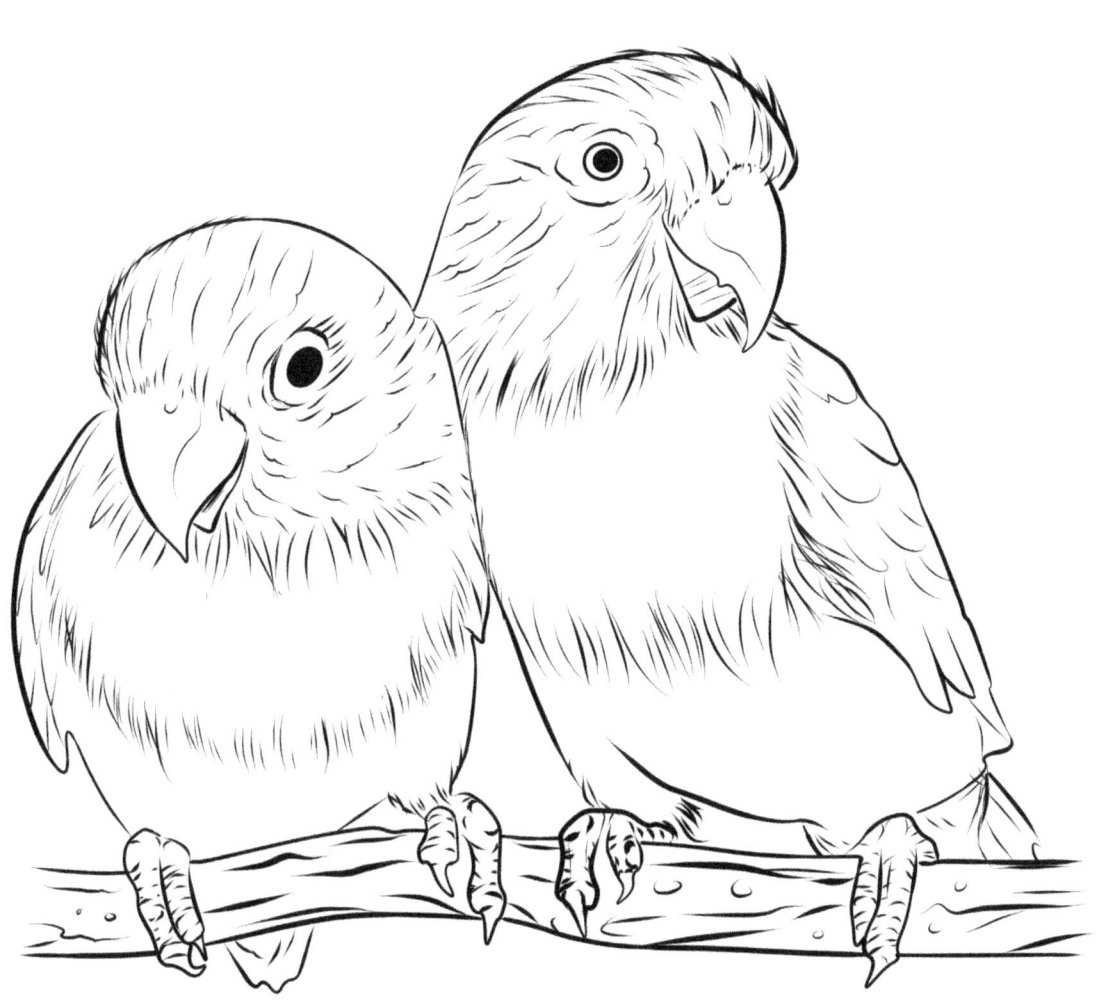

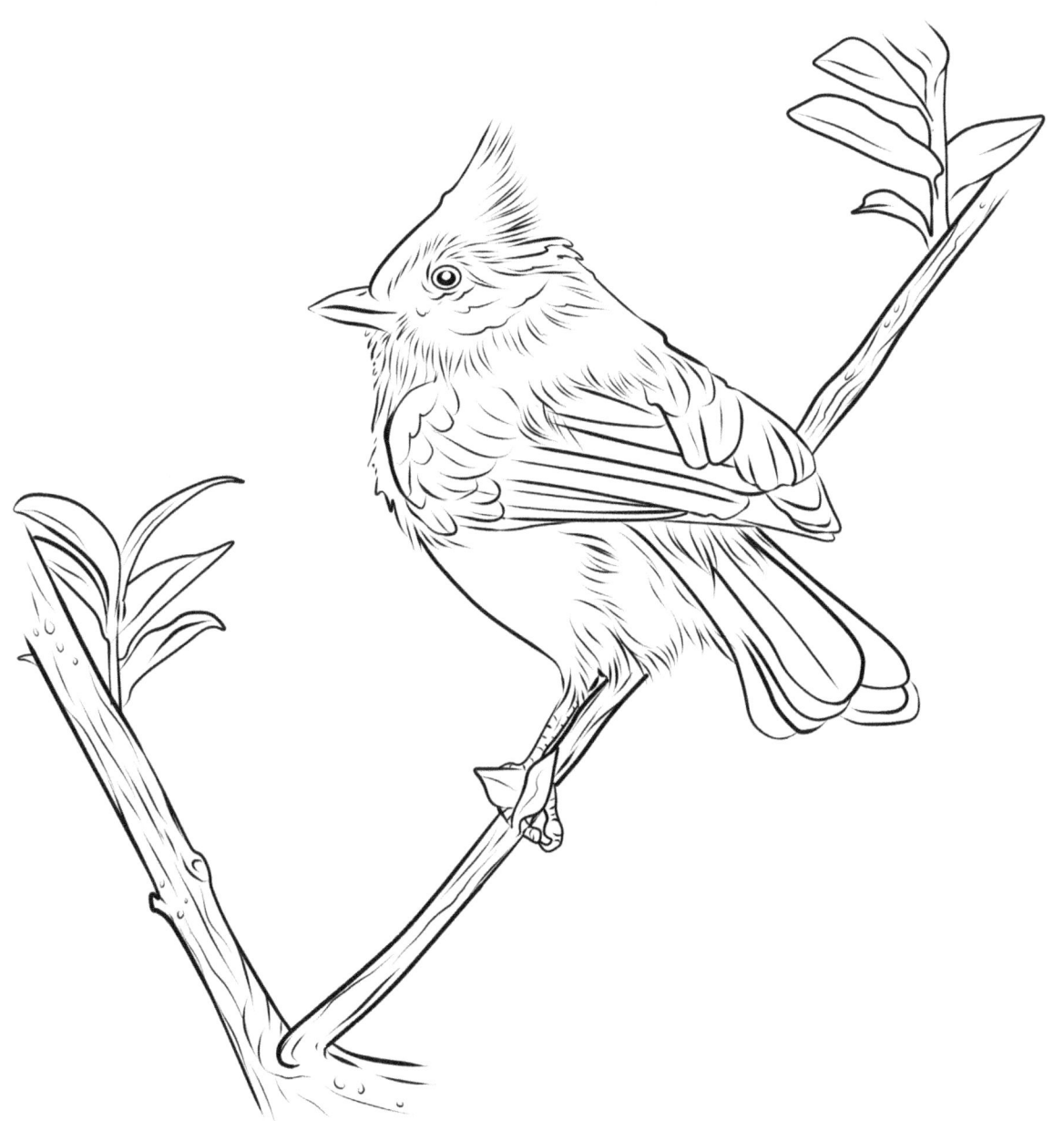

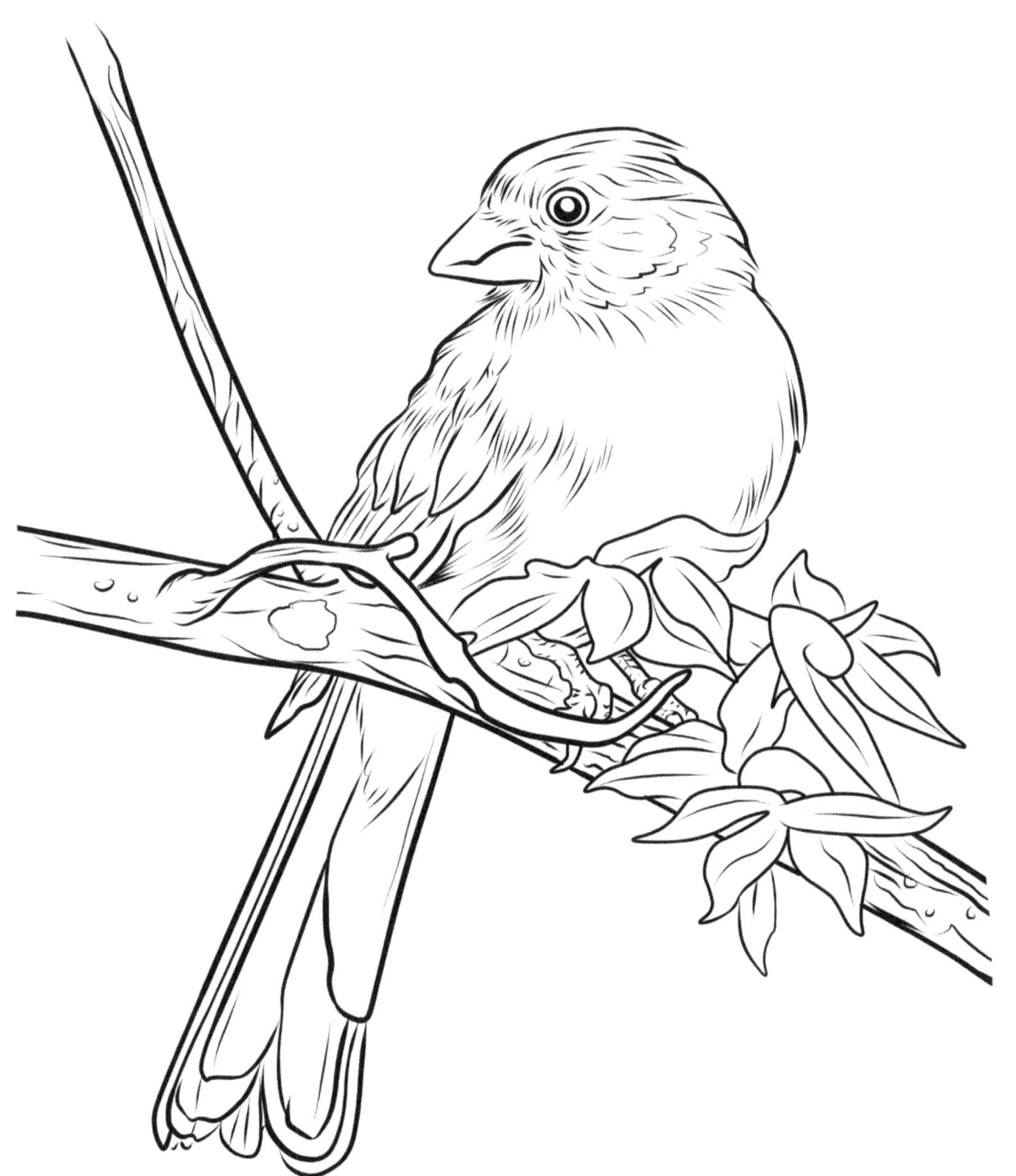

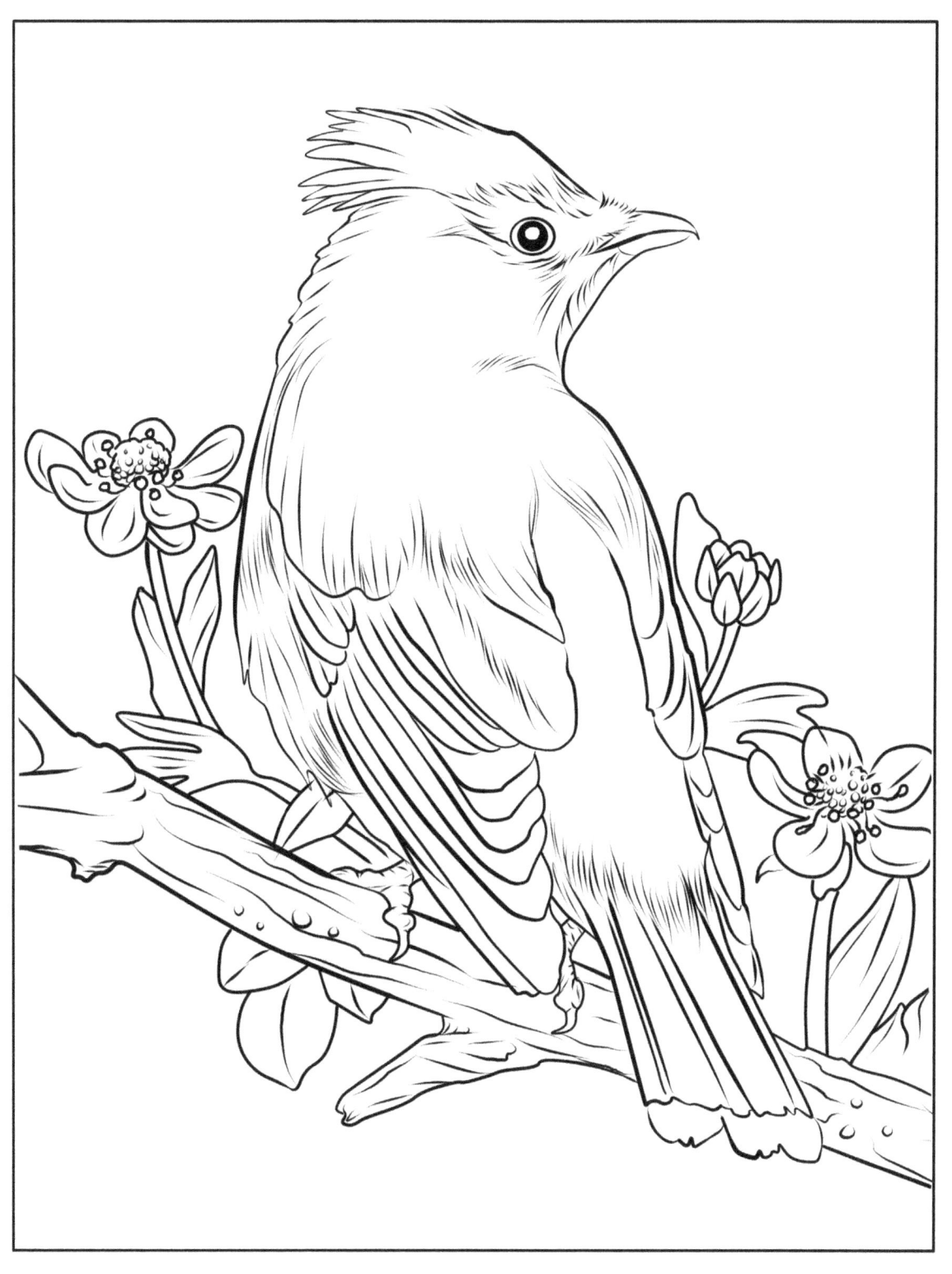

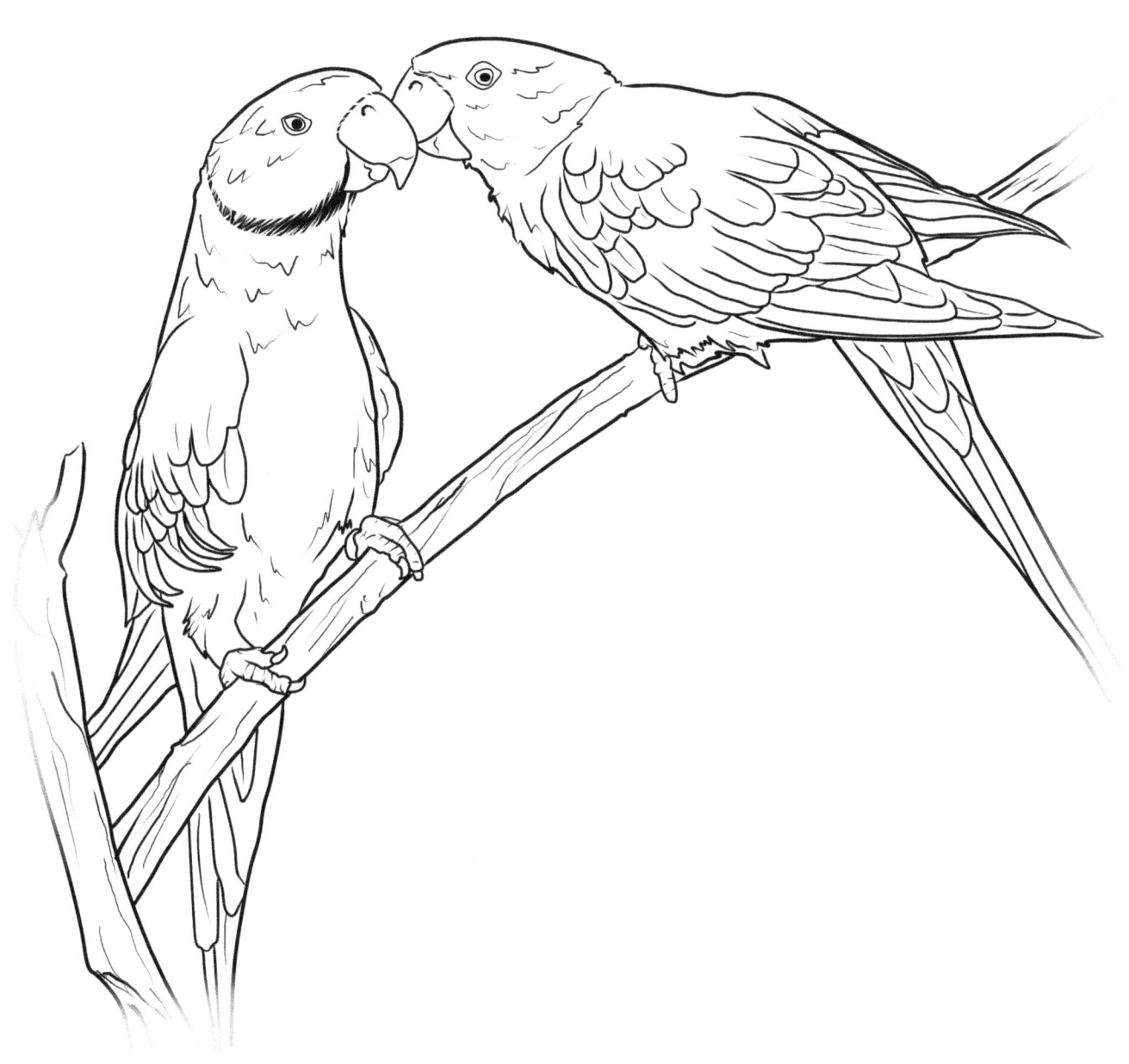

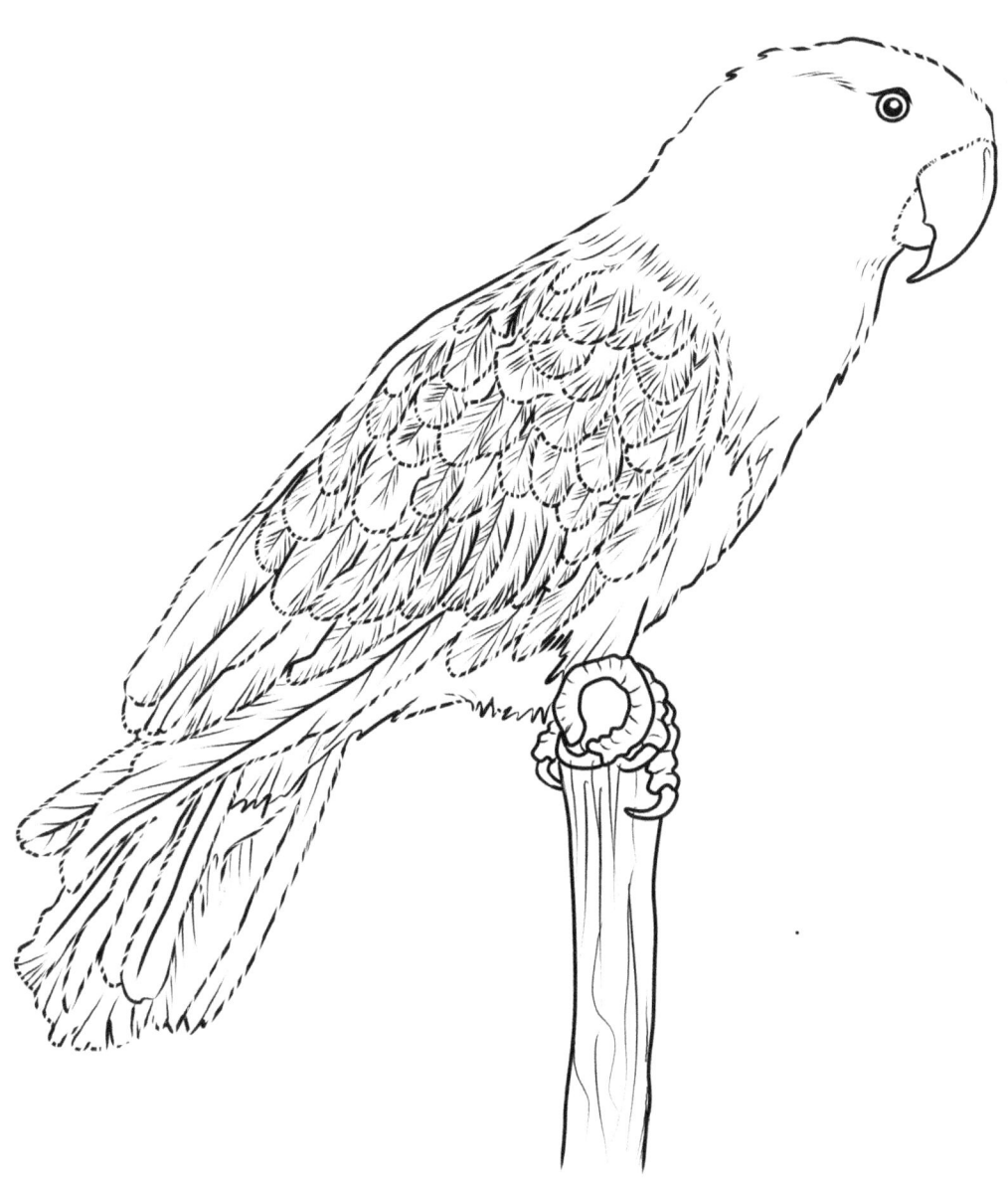

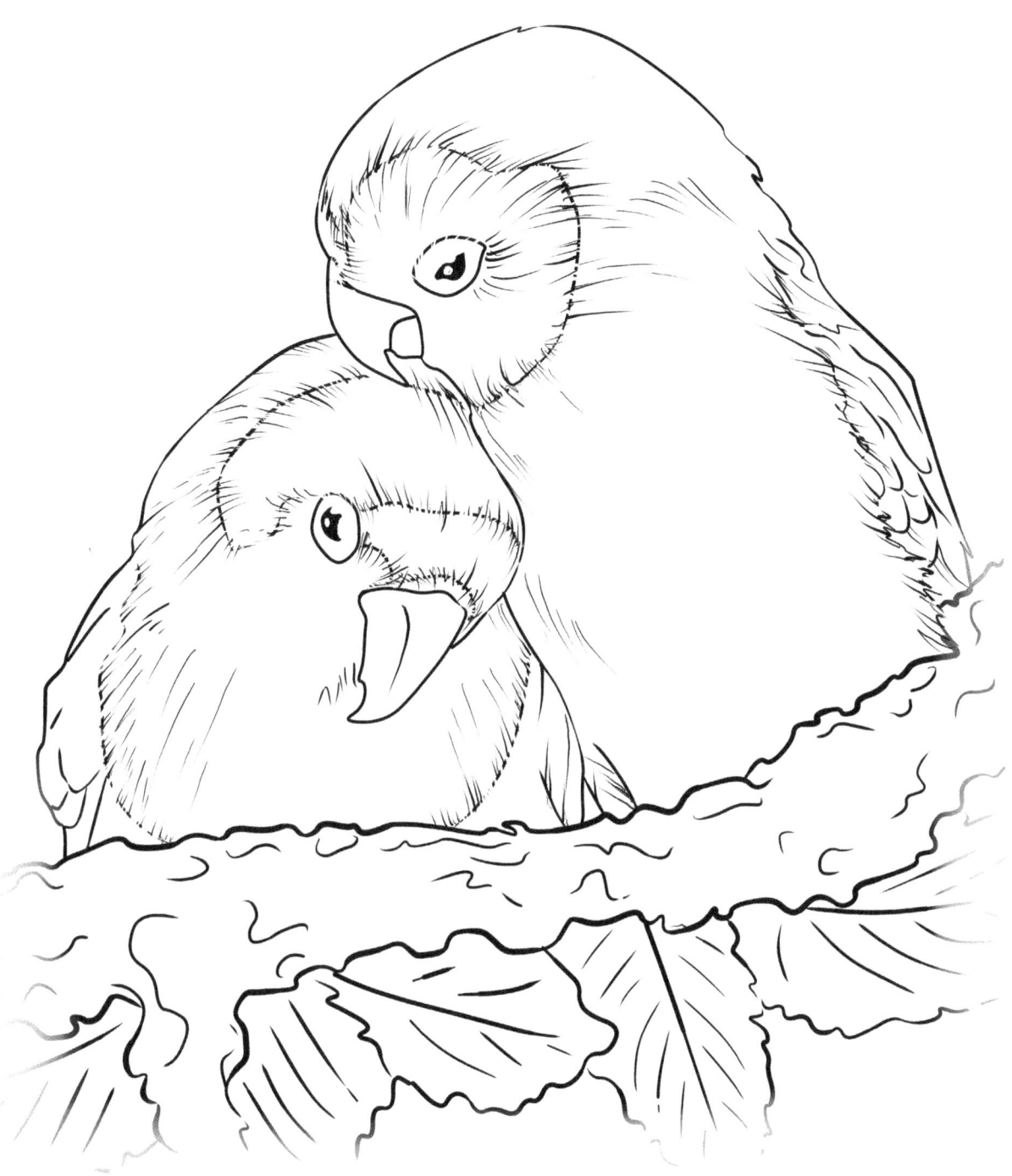

www.ingramcontent.com/pod-product-compliance
Lightning Source LLC
Chambersburg PA
CBHW080605190526
45169CB00007B/2892